Jayson Krause

SEARCH ENGINE OPTIMIZATION

The Ultimate Guide to Successful Search Engine Optimization, Learn Proven Strategies and Practices That Can Ensure Continuous Targeted Traffic to Your Niche Sites

Descrierea CIP a Bibliotecii Naţionale a României
JAYSON KRAUSE
    SEARCH ENGINE OPTIMIZATION. The Ultimate Guide to Successful Search Engine Optimization, Learn Proven Strategies and Practices That Can Ensure Continuous Targeted Traffic to Your Niche Sites / Jayson Krause. – Bucharest: Editura My Ebook, 2020
    ISBN

JAYSON KRAUSE

SEARCH ENGINE OPTIMIZATION

The Ultimate Guide to Successful Search Engine Optimization, Learn Proven Strategies and Practices That Can Ensure Continuous Targeted Traffic to Your Niche Sites

My Ebook Publishing House
Bucharest, 2020

TABLE OF CONTENTS

FOREWORD

What is SEO? It's an abbreviation for Search Engine Optimization. What precisely does SEO do? It's the method of breaking down and constructing individual web pages, as well as whole sites, so that they may be discovered, analyzed, and then indexed by assorted search engines.

SEO may make the material of your web pages more relevant, more magnetic, and more easily read by search engines and their crawling and indexing software.

Why would this be of avid importance to you? Would it be crucial to you if buyers were unable to discover your phone number or find the address of your business? I don't think that many businesses may survive for very long in that situation.

This state of affairs may apply to a site. Can likely buyers locate your current site easily? Traffic to your site may be extremely low. Potential buyers may not even know that your site exists.

Chapter 1

Indexing/Link Building Techniques- Blogging and RSS

Synopsis

We are going to look at are a few techniques to quickly build back links which will successively get your page indexed, in most cases at a pretty speedy pace. If you're already indexed this may further your position in the search engines or drive the search engines to crawl more of your pages and get more of your site indexed. First Blogging and RSS.

Blogs and RSS

Blogging

Blogging is essentially a different way to get back links. Once you compose a blog, Google knows about it practically before you're finished authoring it. Google and additional search engines travel to Blog sites too many times in a day to calculate.

Once you make a blog posting and nonchalantly drop your web site with a link to it, you have in reality produced a back link. Any blog host that's of any worthiness is indexed in Google and Google trusts what these Blog web sites say and if you link to your web site in a Blog you're commonly indexed promptly.

Almost all techniques of getting indexed promptly rely on back links and acquiring them easily. Blogging is an awesome way and so is having your acquaintances link to you who are already indexed.

Below are a few reputable Blog web sites that will be of excellent use to you. Make it a point not to put a blog on every single one or at any rate don't put a blog on every one and utilize the future techniques I'm going to talk about. It'll do more damage than good.

Great sites to Blog about your web site (listed as I believe they should go, they're all good):

- Blogger
- BlogSpot
- 360 Degrees
- MySpace
- Xanga
- LiveJournal
- Multiply
- Opera
- Blog

There are many, many, many more Blogging web sites. A few are for simply general blogs and others are for particular sorts of Blogs. Do a little research and you will discover a lot more with ease.

Blogging blended with Pinging might be the most valuable and successful way to get indexed.

It is all free of charge and all truly great when it comes to getting indexed and getting indexed promptly.

I will get into pinging soon but first of all I wish to touch up on RSS.

RSS

RSS stands for Really Simply Syndication. It is a way to let the search engines and blog hosts recognize when you update your page or blog as soon as it is done. While RSS alone is un-needed, when you make the best of it with your blog or page it's simply a different tool in the arsenal of indexing that you are able to readily make the best of.

Once again, this isn't a comprehensive guide to anything it's simply a way to get you set up and know what you're doing so I'm not going to write page after page on RSS. The matchless neat thing about RSS that I may tell you is that it truly does work.

Everything I've said so far and will work, but RSS is truly simple to accomplish and is simply an add-on to your web site that will help either get you indexed or hold your ranking. There isn't a great deal more to RSS so I'll leave it at that and get to the beefier stuff.

Chapter 2

Indexing/Link Building Techniques-Pinging

Synopsis

Pinging - truly it ought to be blogging and pinging but you'll learn about that later in my step by step design for getting indexed. Rapidly!

Ping It

Pinging is in reality 2 things, it's more than 2 things but in its principal form it may be 2 things.

There's the old school DOS command to ping which will affirm that an I.P. address or site is alive or at any rate accessible thru DOS. Then there's the fairly new technique of Pinging that's a little dissimilar.

The sort of Pinging I'm discussing now is when you're talking about sending word to the search engines about your page and what it's all about. Pinging essentially is telling. Telling the search engines like I said previously.

Once you ping something on the net via a site and not the DOS command you're doing 2 things at a time. You're as a matter of fact telling the site to check your site and see that it exists but you're likewise telling the web site to tell the search engines about your web site.

When your site or page has been pinged (you are able to ping either your page or your entire web site, it's best to do every page one at a time) it lets the search engines recognize you pinged it. Commonly the search engines don't even have to be interested in your page to then index your page founded on somebody (you) pinging it.

Unless you're being observed by the search engines they've no idea it's you pinging the site and not somebody else.

They wish to know about it as they think somebody else wishes to know about your web site.

Search engines are a lot like adolescents. They rate and rank humans based upon other individuals opinions. Now, simply because a lot of individuals ping your page (no one truly will do this because it only helps you and not them in the short-term) it doesn't mean that will assist you.

Ping it and forget it is the phrase I like to live by. Occasionally you'll have the bots crawling all over you like a shot, occasionally it will take a bit longer and occasionally it will be of no use.

Search engines wouldn't be a multi, multi-billion dollar business if everybody recognized precisely how they worked or what makes them tick so let's simply do yourself a favor and not dwell on it and merely do what we know works, like the material contained in this eBook.

Because pinging is such an excellent practice there are tons of sites made to simply ping additional sites. I'll list the sites that ping a lot of sites to let them know about your web site and or page. Here are a few sites you are able to utilize to ping your page or site:

- Pingomatic
- Blogflux
- Google
- King Ping
- Feedshark

- BlogBlip

- PinGates

- PingIn

- AutoPinger

- FeedBurner

As I stated these ping sites in reality utilize additional ping sites to ping your web site. What I mean and what you'll discover is you type your web site and description into the site and then it will take that info and ping anyplace from 5- 50 web sites.

This is partially why I said simply utilize one of these sites as it's really pinging your web site a lot more than just once in many cases.

Like the blog sites, you are able to easily discover sites to ping your web site with for indexing purposes I simply listed a couple of them here that are long-familiar and well- thought-of.

Chapter 3

Indexing/Link Building Techniques-PPC

Synopsis

PPC as you know is where you pay the search engines a fee each time somebody clicks your ad and brings a potential customer to your web site. While this is great to advertise with (not awesome), it's a great way to get a fresh web site indexed rapidly.

Pay Per Click

If you've utilized Adwords in the last few years you will understand that clicks may easily be a couple of dollars apiece.

For the more competitory niches clicks may be hundreds of dollars. Who would ever pay that for one click is beyond me, unless a major corporation is doing something.

For the aim of indexing though it doesn't truly matter if you have to pay say $5.00 for a click as you only need one click to your ad for this little magic trick to work. There's a list of great PPC sites below however first let me explain how this works if you haven't already garnered that by now.

Let's suppose you are kicking upstairs "auto insurance in Phoenix, Arizona". Really quick though, that example niche is an awesome illustration of a long tail keyword. It's really to the point and not across-the-board at all. Anyways, back to what I was talking about.

What you wish to do is produce a PPC campaign at any of the PPC sites listed below or anyplace. Bid as high or low as you wish as we're not concerned with the caliber of the visit. We simply require a visit from an outside source.

Watch the campaign cautiously. If the keyword price is pretty depressed then by all means spend a couple of clams acquiring a few clicks. When the search engines discover these clicks they think they're of high quality and interesting as they're being sent to you by their own site, the search engine. The search engines aren't bright enough to understand what is really going on. There's nothing illegal or anything about this exercise.

It's not the speediest way to get indexed but it will get you indexed much speedier than simply placing your site or page up and waiting indexing. In my own experience this technique takes a couple of days at most and is directly associated to having your web site advertised on the search engine.

The search engines aren't being decent to you as you advertised, they're simply seeing somebody searching for something and then seeing your web site appear. It doesn't know if your web site is "by nature" in the site or a "pay for placement" listing.

Recall I told you search engines like popular sites, if somebody searches and discoveries you it believes your web site is popular and you simply got a huge jump start on the entire procedure. In essence and many times in actuality you are able to pay a couple of cents to get indexed. If you are able to get merely one of the keywords you wish to rank for, for a couple of cents a click say $0.10 (10 cents and I know this is occasionally rare but bare with me) you may achieve 100 visits to your web site.

This is good in 2 ways. You have a hundred real visitors who are really interested in your web site and they might purchase whatever you're selling but likewise you have a hundred visits to your web site that the search engines are going to see.

If you simply place the page up and did the PPC ad not long after that the search engines will see your site as pretty popular. It might only be popular on one web site but who cares, it's a beginning and the engines feed off of one another.

To put this tactic in to use, listed below are a fistful of beneficial PPC sites:

- Miva

- MSN

- Marchex

- Google

As with anything on the net there are tons of pay-per-click sites and services also. Ask around, see what others are utilizing and simply make certain the PPC site is legit.

Remember the chief focus of this isn't choice visitors, simply plain old visitors. While it's great to get visitors who require what you're giving them, we simply want the search engines to see that individuals are searching, discovering you and visiting you. The popularity competition is ceaseless.

Chapter 4

Indexing/Link Building Techniques- Social Bookmarking

Synopsis

The birth and boom of Social Bookmarking is moderately fresh but so is its effect on Link building which is in the final analysis plays a big role in either getting indexed or sustaining your status with the search engine(s).

Social Bookmarking web sites are a sort of net community. Members of the SB (Social Bookmarking) web sites have the power and authority to recommend and or vote on sites that are put forward by other users of the community.

Social Sites

They're essentially a search engine but the sites that come up in its Index (yes, it's really similar to a "plain old" search engines") or directory are handpicked from a lot of submissions and or advocated by additional users of the community.

Google and most additional huge search engines hold SB sites on a whole other level.

They greatly regard and value what the SB sites think or simply list. As Google pays attention to what the SB sites are up to as far as the listings go, all you require is a single link from a SB site and you're gold in Google's eyes.

Social Bookmarking sites let their users (you) "tag" the submissions. Tags are essentially keywords for your submission. You ought to attempt and utilize the same keywords you utilized in your META tags for your SB submissions.

All you have to carry out is submit your web site to one or several of the Social Bookmarking web sites to get indexed rapidly. No one has to vote or advocate your web site, the SB site simply has to recognize it and really quickly the search engines will recognize it as well.

Check into a couple of these Social Bookmarking web sites:

- Propeller
- Digg
- Del.icio.us
- Tagza
- Newsvine
- Swik
- Blinklist
- Mister-Wong
- Backflip

So visit a few of the above web sites and submit your sites or utilize a free of charge service like Social Marker to submit your page to a lot of SB sites at one time. The more sites you submit to the better, to a point. Do not go crazy however if you submit to 5 or 10 sites you have 5 or 10 more possible exposures in Google.

Inside a couple of hours occasionally sooner there's a really, very great chance submitted pages will turn up in Google's Index or results page. If you're not listed straight off in Google, do not fret. Some of the times it may take up to 2 days to get listed thru this technique but short of having a back link from an already indexed web site with a high page rank this is the fastest technique.

Chapter 5

Indexing/Link Building Techniques- Articles

Synopsis

Articles are a different awesome way to get back links. Before the days of Social Bookmarking and sites like MySpace and the blog sites, Articles were a key part to getting indexed.

With all the fresh developments on the net, a few individuals over look Articles as a marketing and indexing source.

Perhaps if you simply want to market via articles you're not going to do well but you're not looking to promote with Articles.

The articles for our aims are for indexing. You'll make the cash after you're indexed and you'll have a much bigger audience with a search engine than you will with an article directory.

Writing

So with articles you get 2 awesome things.

One being traffic from the article viewers but even more significantly you'll acquire the much desired attention from the search engines as a direct outcome of having your page on an article web site. It's very easy to glean the rewards of articles.

As with any other technique of getting back links, you'll need to submit your article to a lot of the article directory sites.

I'll give you a few great places to post your articles in a minute but first of all I wish to tell you how to compose a great article.

Much like your page requires a few central things for success, your article will require a couple of central ingredients to glean the rewards of articles. Each article submission and directory site lets you submit your own article. Among the most significant things to remember is to make certain the article is really yours or if you "acquired ideas" from another article, make certain to totally rewrite the article in your own words.

Most articles are simply copies of one another if you're discussing the same subject but you'll always be able to add your own views and input to it. Just like the search engines don't like repeat or copied material; neither do the article sites, so simply make certain you're submitting your own work.

The following thing you're going to have to capitalize on is the 'resource box'. The resource box is virtually what it sounds like. It's a little box on the page where your article comes out. This little box bears pertinent info about you and your material.

You'll have to include your name in the material. You are able to utilize a pen or stage name, simply make it consistent. When the same name is submitting material it will produce a sense of authority or notoriety.

The address of your site or web page is likewise really crucial. Without this data the whole article is worthless for SEO and Indexing purposes. If you wish to go off on a tangent and simply write and write with no return then by all means do it, however I'm into getting something back for my sweat.

"Pitching" your product is likewise something you'll need to do in the resource box. It's simply a one- three sentence, powerfully to the point description of what you're providing.

Why should somebody read your article? Well, you have to assure them and you assure them in the resource box.

A call to action is likewise a really great element to any article or resource box. Most of the marketing is really done in the resource box and not the material itself. The article is merely something you have to have.

The primary idea and goal behind the material is really what's in the resource box. As I stated it will have your name, URL, pitch, and call to action. If you're writing on dog food and you happen to be marketing dog food then make your call to action stick out and make the reader travel to your site.

Even if you don't achieve a visit, you still have a link on a highly ranked page and in turn Google and the search engines will consume your site.

All of these techniques so far are not necessarily a way to achieve direct traffic however a way to get your link dropped and linked to the web site that's already one of Google's favorites. You are able to get started authoring a quick and to the point article of about four hundred words and post it to a few of the article sites below.

- Ezine Articles
- Go Articles
- Article Dashboard
- Article Biz
- Article Alley
- Forums

Lots of individuals visit and utilize forums on a steady basis. More significantly most reputable, long-familiar forums have been around for a while. Google loves when a site has been indexed for a while and has stayed in the index for more than a couple of weeks or months.

There are forums on virtually every topic out there. From animal lovers to xylophone fanciers, if you search for a forum, you'll discover it. You ought to find a forum that has a couple of thousand members and is easily discovered in the search engines.

Forums are a few of the last and few niche avenues of marketing. Even on big social networking and bookmarking sites like MySpace and Digg they might have forums but there's never just a basic forum.

There are constantly different themed or inched topics for forum posting. This is an awesome thing for getting back links from a site on your subject, to your site. Relevancy is likewise a factor in getting your site in to the SERP.

If individuals are interested in your page, commonly the search engines are interested in your page. If you have a link in your key signature on a forum post you did, Google and the other SE's most likely don't know you really did the post with the link in it.

On a side note, you ought to attempt and avoid really making a post with the link right in the post. Rather, do a couple of posts but make certain to include a link to your site in your signature. Reciprocally this link will appear each time you make a post.

Be cautious not to post too much or simply create random posts to drop your link. The SE's don't truly care about this but the BBSs themselves do. If they ban your account and or I.P. address before you get indexed it's simply a waste and you might have ruined your shot at feeding off the power of BBS posts.

As there are millions of forums out there I'm not going to waste your time with a list of forums. A awesome way to discover a niche particular forum is to Google and in the search box put in the word "forum" followed by a "+" and then the niche or topic you wish to discover a forum for.

Chapter 5

Indexing/Link Building Techniques- Press Release

Synopsis

In addition to the previous techniques, a different great way to get a back link from a reputable site in Google's' eyes is to utilize a press release.

A press release isn't only a nice and simple way to acquire quality back links which will get you a quality indexing job by the search engines, but it's an awesome way to acquire some true traffic.

Announcing

Not too many years ago having a press release typically implied have a publicist and or you being somebody who individuals would be interested in right off the bat.

Individuals adore news. Naturally, individuals are really gossipy.

The biggest television and radio networks on the globe are, you got it, news show networks. Fox, CNN, ABC, NBC, etc... The old days of media are on the way out and have been for a while.

Naturally individuals still read the papers and watch the news on television. As a matter of fact there's millions of individuals who don't even utilize the net. There are however more individuals who utilize the net than individuals who don't utilize the net.

No matter whether they utilize the net as a news source it will still do its task of marketing you and or getting you indexed, pretty rapidly as well.

It takes simply a couple of individuals to see your press release before everybody, both on and offline will know about whatsoever you wish them to know. Why shouldn't individuals be discussing you? There's no reason.

For instance a band today may compose their own press release and introduce themselves to the world thru the net. It didn't used to be like that however. The Beetles didn't visit a site, submit a little info and become a household name just like that. Just, they may have if they weren't in the 1960's.

With the advent of the net you no longer have to have rich pockets, acquaintances in elevated places or truly anything more than a PC with net access to make news. You are able to easily let the whole net learn about you, your product or service or truly anything you want.

A publicist and a pro author are no longer required however. Press releases are nothing more than a way of self marketing. Putting down press releases wasn't my aim here. What I mean is the aim of any press release is to market.

It's not something as easy as 'Visit This Site and Purchase' but the entire aim of a press release is to call attention to an individual, place or thing, you merely do it in the 3rd person and add a little personality to it.

You need the viewer's attention as you need to attempt to finally sell them something. Press releases on the net may and will get you back links but it's among the few affairs that may get you indexed and get a little true traffic to your site so it's a win-win state of affairs.

The entire press release thing might frighten you away merely as it has the word Press in it.

Anybody who can write a couple of sentences or paragraphs may now produce an impressive and enlivening press release that might be seen and acted on by millions of individuals.

Many Press Release sites cost a little cash to use the service but there are a few free PR sites that will still do an awesome job. Remember, a PR site will get you indexed but likewise get you constant attention.

These PR sites are an excellent place to see other press releases to learn from and then submit your own:

- PR Web
- Free Press Release
- PR Free
- Press Releases
- 24/7 Press Release

Wrapping Up

Simply having a site is no longer what you have to have to succeed. Today, you not only require a great website, you need individuals to come to your site and you need to be able to compete with all the other individuals who are doing what you're doing. It's a numbers pool and there are lots of individuals looking for and supplying info.

It is not always simple to dominate the search engines however if you are able to simply achieve a little attention from them today, more and more attention will come after and that may only translate into one matter. Traffic. Not simply random traffic but targeted traffic. From my own knowledge there is no greater traffic than "natural" or "organic" traffic end of story.

Make yourself stick out and rise to the top of the SERP. Simply think, there is a great chance you did not even know what SEO or SERP or anything I've brought up in this material was. However you're now a much better net marketer by simply having this knowledge.

It is up to you to go out there and achieve getting your pages and sites Indexed and turn into an SEO Guru.

Well perhaps not a GURU but at least you are able to at long last put Google and the other Search Engines on your squad and allow them to do all the work for you.

9 786069 836583

Printed by Libri Plureos GmbH in Hamburg, Germany